The Timpson Way

First published in 2004 by Timpson Limited.

ISBN 0-9547049-0-8

Timpson House Claverton Road Wythenshawe Manchester M23 9TT
Tel: 0161 946 6200 www.timpson.com

Written by John Timpson. Printed in Great Britain.

How to increase your bonus

Our top bonus earners show what can be achieved, it's a list of ordinary individuals who can create incredible results. If they can do it, so can everyone else. If you want to earn more money read on.

Biggest bonus earners

Expert Advice

Big bonuses don't arrive by luck, they come from hard work. All the experts say an individual can have a big influence on his own bonus. It's not just a question of working harder, often the best results are achieved by working smarter. No one is excluded, everyone can learn how to improve their bonus earnings. It doesn't matter who you are or what you look like, young, old, black, white, tall or small, men and women, everyone can learn to earn a bigger bonus.

What the experts say

Learning from experience

We decided the only way to discover how to earn a bigger bonus was to ask those people who are already earning lots of money. We tracked down the best people earning the biggest bonus and studied their performance. This book contains the tips we were taught by the Timpson experts.

Anyone can learn

Our Bonus Book

How to increase your bonus

The Timpson Way

Getting the buzz

As soon as you walk into a shop you sense the atmosphere. Often it's buzzy and business like, but some shops can be cold and unfriendly. Customers notice the vibes, that's why happy shops earn the biggest bonuses.

A happy shop with BUZZ!

Pick your mood

Have you noticed some people make life fun while others ruin your day. Just look a doom merchant in the face first thing in the morning and you know what's coming for the rest of the day. If you notice other people's moods, they notice yours. Remember, Mr Grumpy doesn't earn big bonuses. Pick your attitude before the day starts. Make sure you put on a good mood before reaching work.

GRUMPY
BORED
CHEERFUL
HELPFUL
DON'T CARE
AMBITIOUS
UNINTERESTED
KEEN
CHEERFUL
ATTITUDE TREE
TIMPSON
BUZZ SIGN
Choose your attitude

Problem People

Let me introduce you to two people to avoid. 'Mr Gunner' and 'Mr Ahbutt.' They both stand in the way of progress whilst pretending to be helpful. 'Mr Ahbutt' always has a reason why things can't be done. He is the first to find a pitfall and the last to solve a problem. 'Mr Gunner' is more enthusiastic, he agrees with what you say and claims he will help, but he never does, all talk and no action, that's 'Mr Gunner.'

MR GUNNER
MR AHBUTT
TIMPSON
TIMPSON
BUZZ SIGN
Don't be negative

Positive People

If you want to earn a big bonus surround yourself with positive people. For some retailers the priority is location, location and location. That's not true at Timpson. Our success depends on the people working inside, it's the personalities that count. A buzzy shop is full of buzzy bodies.

TIMPSON
TIMPSON
BUZZ SIGN
A buzzy shop is full of buzzy bodies

Happiness Helps

If you don't enjoy working here let us know. If we can't make you happy you are better working somewhere else. You spend a large chunk of your life at work, so find a job you enjoy. We like people who love coming to work.

SIGN OF A BUZZY SHOP

Think of the money

There is no shame in being greedy, with our bonus scheme, you deserve all that you can get. We want people who work with us to create a better lifestyle. We like people who want to earn big money.

SIGN OF A BUZZY SHOP

BUZZ SIGN

Be greedy

Art of the possible

We like people who say "No problem," the shops that take most money turn few customers away, they try to tackle every job. Success comes to ambitious people who find ways to make things happen.

SIGN OF A BUZZY SHOP

You really are in charge

The Timpson "Upside-down Management" style means you really can make a difference. Nothing stops you testing the ideas you believe will make more money. You have the freedom to develop the business and create the biggest possible bonus.

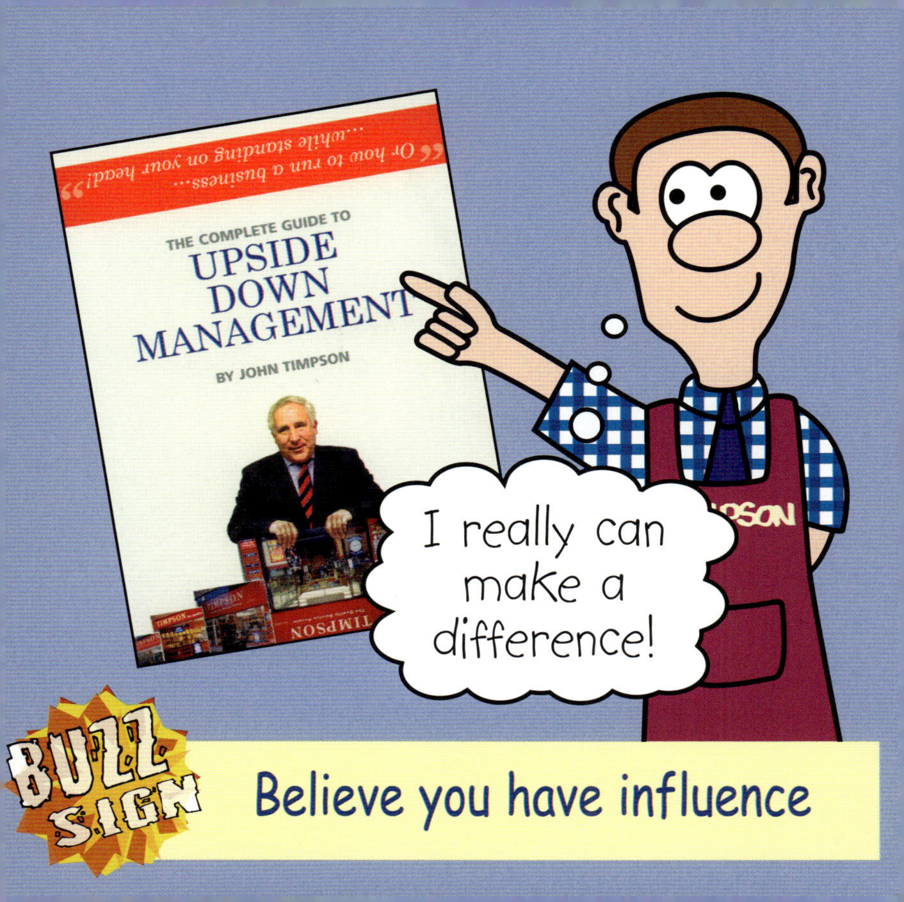

"Or how to run a business...
...while standing on your head!"
THE COMPLETE GUIDE TO
UPSIDE DOWN MANAGEMENT
BY JOHN TIMPSON
I really can make a difference!
BUZZ SIGN
Believe you have influence

Turnover is created

Satisfactory service puts money in the till but won't make you a superstar. There is a big difference between average and great performance. In our shops you can create lots of extra turnover. Find ways to increase sales and benefit your bonus.

A GOOD MANAGER CAN INCREASE SALES BY 65%!
MANAGER
TIMPSON
QUESTION?
WHAT IS THE MOST MONEY YOU HAVE TAKEN IN A WEEK?
BUZZ SIGN
Believe you can increase sales

A day at a time

Look forward to every new day, you don't know what is going to happen. There is often a new challenge, especially if you set yourself targets. It's satisfying to go home with a sense of achievement, especially if you earn a bigger bonus.

BUZZ SIGN

Make each day a challenge

Well Informed

Good people always know how well they are doing. They know last years sales and how much they have taken today. They even sense the very moment when they pass their target and it won't take them long to calculate their bonus.

So far £220 up on last week and £420 helps to make £3000 which will get me £92 bonus!
TIMPSON
BUZZ SIGN
Know the score

Have a laugh

Business is serious but you should have fun while you do it. You don't make money by being miserable, that puts off the customers and annoys your colleagues. Make someone laugh everyday, it will help you earn lots of bonus.

Happy Birthday Ken
GUESS HIS AGE
TIMPSON
There's £5 if you win, all profits go to charity
TIMPSON
HAVE FUN !!
BUZZ SIGN

Get stuck in

Successful people give their personal commitment to the business. That doesn't mean being a workaholic, but sometimes you must go the extra mile and turn up for work when feeling under the weather. At Timpson you are part of a team, you are involved in our successes and our failure - you are totally involved with Timpson not just when you feel like it.

Just popped in to see how you are doing!
Can't you keep away on your day off?
TIMPSON
TIMPSON
BUZZ SIGN
Be involved
VITAL
NO SICKIES!

No Hesitation

Successful people act immediately. If something has to be done, they do it straight away. If they have an idea, they give it a go. If someone needs some help, they get on and do it. Life is so much easier if you get on with it.

TIMPSON
Just take a seat, I'll be as quick as I can.
BUZZ SIGN
DO IT NOW !!

Be an all rounder

Single job experts seldom make big bonuses at Timpson. You can't make money through just one service. A long time ago, cobblers had to learn to cut keys, now they must also repair watches and do engraving. By serving every customer that comes through the door they have become big bonus earners.

DIPLOMA
DIPLOMA
DIPLOMA
DIPLOMA
TIMPSON
BUZZ SIGN
Be multiskilled

Continuous Improvement

If your ambition is to stand still you will stagnate. You must always want to improve and keep setting yourself new goals. However good you are, you can always get better.

When can I take level 4?
Must beat Selfridges!
TIMPSON
BUZZ SIGN
Aim to get better

Take up the challenge

You won't earn a bigger bonus by sitting on the fence, take up the challenge of new training, difficult jobs and achieving extra sales. Active people with a spirit of adventure can earn big money, it pays to have a go.

BUZZ SIGN

Have a go !

First things first

No one can do everything at once, so spend your time doing things that really matter. In some businesses the priority is to please your boss, with us it's different, we ask you to make our customers happy. That will increase our turnover, your bonus and incidentally will indeed please your boss.

BUZZ SIGN

Know your priorities

Built in time table

Develop the ability to quote the quickest time for each job. Ideally, everything is done 'While You Wait,' but at peak times that isn't possible. Clever colleagues always know the work in progress and quote the best time with confidence. They visualise a work schedule in their mind.

1 HEEL JOBS - 5 min
2 KEY ORDERS - 5 min
3 PET TAGS - 40 min
4 THROUGH SOLE - 1 hour
5 NEW HEEL - 2 days
BUZZ SIGN
Have a schedule in your mind

Spread Enjoyment

Selfish people don't realise how others react to their personality, they are too interested in themselves to bother. You earn a big bonus by bringing a smile to the customers' faces to make them feel special. They spend more money if you make their day.

Make their day !

Ready for the rush

When your shop gets busy, nothing must get in the way of looking after customers. You can't afford to worry if you have got the right stock or whether the machine is going to work. Be ready for the rush, start each day as you mean to go on.

TIMPSON
WHILE YOU WAIT SERVICE
BUZZ SIGN
Be prepared

Great start to the day

Make sure your shop standards are perfect, every night, before you go home. That's the way to give yourself a great start the following day.

BUZZ SIGN
Perfect start to the day

Food for thought

When planning the day ahead, don't forget yourself. In particular, don't forget food. A butty box of goodies brought from home is always better than McDonalds.

It's your favourite lunch!
LUNCH BOX
TIMPSON
BUZZ SIGN
Bring a butty box

Tea Boy

The machinery might run on electricity but a lot of our shops run on tea. Make sure you have plenty of tea bags, sugar and milk before you start your day's work.

SUNRISE DAIRY
M350
Sunrise Dairy Milk
Sunrise Dairy
TIMPSON
BUZZ SIGN

Buy the milk

Early Bird

Good managers arrive well before the opening time displayed on the door. A few minutes spent putting everything in place before you open can save lots of time and create more turnover throughout the day.

TIMPSON
Service People
KEYS
Household
Car
BUZZ SIGN
Arrive early

Unclaimed Repairs

Cobblers with a pile of unfinished repairs on the counter, don't take much money. If you store work for the days ahead, you will be piling up trouble. The secret of a busy shop is to tackle jobs 'While You Wait.'

Why don't you offer a 'while you wait' service?
TIMPSON
BUZZ SIGN
Don't build up trouble

Early opening hours

Our door sticker promises we will be open on time. But if you are ready to open early, don't keep customer's waiting, put their money in the till.

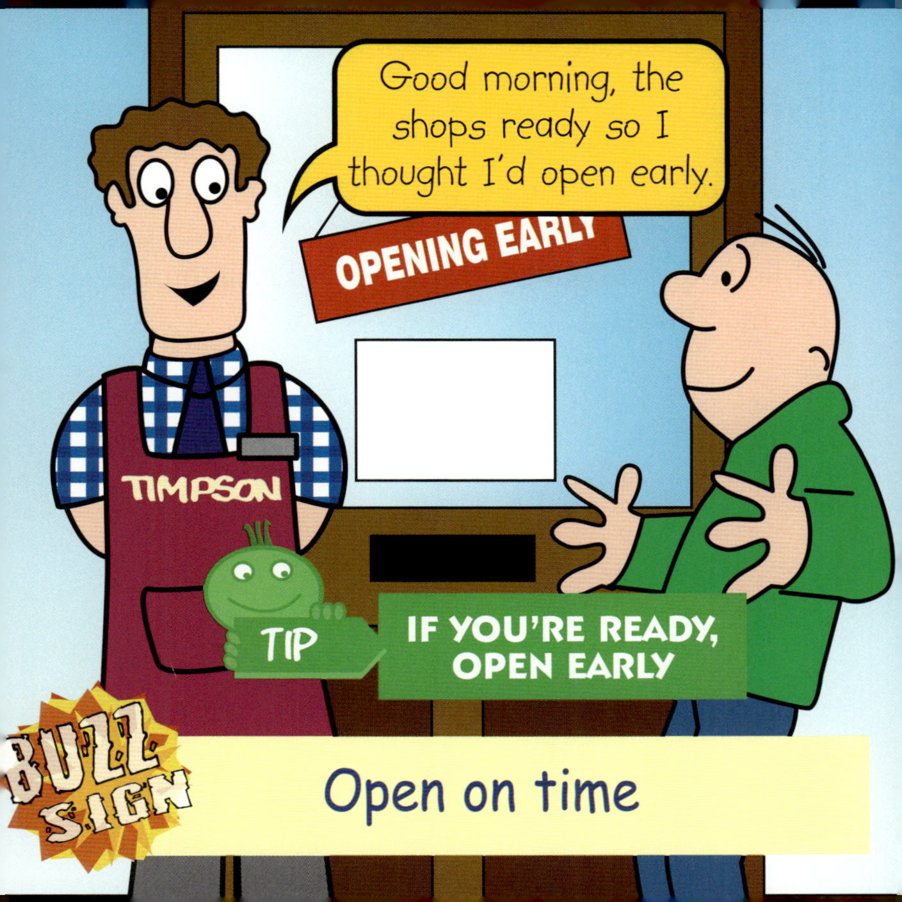
Good morning, the shops ready so I thought I'd open early.
OPENING EARLY
TIMPSON
TIP
IF YOU'RE READY, OPEN EARLY
BUZZ SIGN
Open on time

First of the day

Make sure everything is prepared for your first customer. They don’t want to be kept waiting while you put change in the till and switch on the machines.

Check the key machines

Presolution soles

3 2 1 0 1 2 3
0 1 2
TIMPSON
Centre the engraver

Off peak tasks

Loads of jobs can be done when customers aren't around. They are the tasks that make sure everything is O.K. when customers arrive. Plan your slack periods to keep on top of the work.

Quiet time jobs

Plan your routine

Even the busiest shops have a quiet time during the week when few customers appear. Take advantage, by scheduling the jobs that are best done when you are surrounded by peace and quiet.

Know your peaks

QUIET TIME JOBS

Cleaning

QUIET TIME JOBS

Paperwork

The right order

Most High Street multiples use computers to run their stock control. We think it's better to trust the people in our shops to decide what merchandise and materials they stock. You know your own business better than any computer. Placing the right orders needs careful thought. This is your most important quiet time job.

QUIET TIME JOBS

Ordering

Time to teach

Training is our best investment for the future, and most of our training is in the shop not in the class room. A lot can be learned while serving customers, but trainees and trainers must use quiet times to develop new skills.

QUIET TIME JOBS

Training

Learning from each other

The people in our shops have found loads of time saving shortcuts. The next few pages show some top tips that give more time to serve customers.

GOOD IDEAS !

Use your reserves

You take a lot of trouble creating good displays, particularly for engravable merchandise. Don't disturb your display to make a sale, whenever possible sell from your stock room.

Sell from the stock room

Up front fee

The phrase "would you like to pay now?" puts money straight in the till and saves you time when the customer returns to collect the job.

Straight in the till

Careful Notes

Keep a diary, it can save a lot of anguish. A record of future plans, past events and memory joggers makes your shop much more efficient and gives you peace of mind.

Use the diary

Simple Files

Disorganised managers can get buried in paper. Admin is an annoying but necessary task to be kept in its place. That place is the black box, designed to make sure you always know where you are with the paperwork.

Use the black box

Tactics

At Timpson everyone mucks and takes their fair share of the good and the dirty jobs. Create a plan to ensure everyone knows their role from one week to the next.

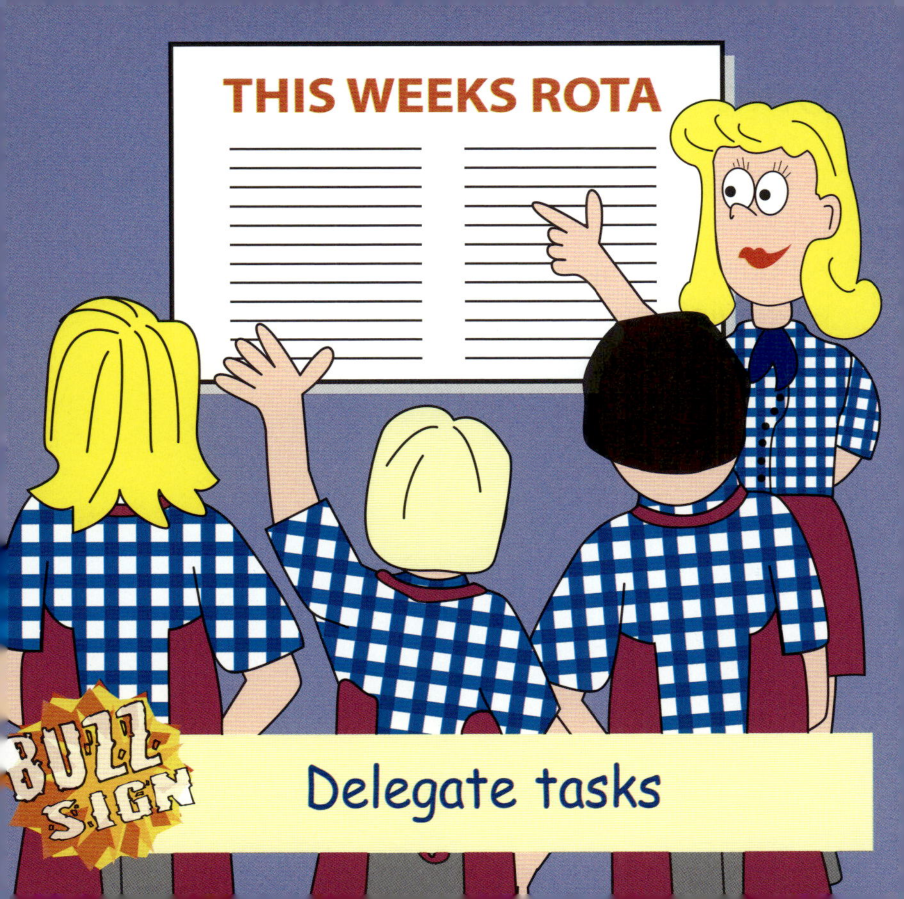
THIS WEEKS ROTA
BUZZ SIGN
Delegate tasks

Shut the stable door

Even the best shops get complaints, particularly on keys. Often the fault lies with the machine. All our equipment requires regular maintenance, everything must be checked following a complaint.

Check machines after every complaint

Don't Delay

High achievers do things immediately. Why bother to write a reminder, when it is so much easier to do the task straight away. 'Do it now' is the best efficiency method ever invented.

SECRET REVEALED
OPEN TO REVEAL THE TOP SALES TIP!
DO IT NOW!
BUZZ SIGN
Best efficiency device ever

Stock Crisis

If you are desperately short of stock, don't waste time wondering how it happened, pick up the 'phone and order the stock you need. The warehouse will supply you with anything you want, we don't want you to lose sales and lose bonus.

Emergency orders

Customer Care

If you need to place a special order, pick up the 'phone while the customer is in the shop. It's the easiest way to order stock and the best way to impress the customer.

SPECIALS

Talking to the experts

The sooner you place your order with an Excellence Centre, the quicker the job will be done. Our Excellence Centres can do the job quicker than any competitor, you can speed up the process by placing the order as soon as it is received. (Don't forget to 'phone Omega straight away.)

Excellence centres

Early Orders

Make sure you have the right merchandise and materials to take the money. Don't order at the last minute, take your time and catch the proper posting date.

Order on time

Action Stations

Don't put off the jobs highlighted on an area visit report. Research shows that jobs not completed within a week are never done. A visit report details things which can take more money. Deal with them straight away, take more money and keep the Area Manager off your back.

Action visit report

Melt Down

If the shop organisation falls apart, desperate measures are called for. Don't patch up trouble in a piece meal way, do it properly, even if that means closing the shop. Return everything to the proper Timpson standard and make it much easier to take money and earn a bigger bonus.

Desperate measures

Help is required

A major shop makeover requires a team effort, you can't do it on your own. Recruit extra help from your area team and make sure the operation is well planned before you start.

Total revamp

No Hurry

Don't worry about working to a deadline, it's better to get your shop absolutely right rather than worrying about business lost while the work is going on. Take time to make sure that the finished job is perfect.

Come back in a week and you'll see an amazing difference.
TIMPSON

Take time

Saturday night Sunday morning

Most shop refits start on a Saturday night, that way we avoid losing business. You should do the same with a major revamp. It's so much easier to work when there are no customers around.

Work nights and sundays

Priorities

You can be so close to your own shop you can't see the problem. Use our check list to make sure your shop is organised to take the money.

6 MAJOR THINGS THAT HELP TAKE MONEY

RIGHT STOCK

MACHINES WORK

WORK UP TO DATE

PAPERWORK TIDY

NO RUBBISH

NO CLUTTER

CHECK LIST

The art of conversation

You must be good at talking to take money. Many shop keepers never speak to you, they are check out clerks, not salesmen. If you want to earn a big bonus you have to speak properly. The following pages show some of the words to use.

The most important job is on the counter!
How do you do, how can I help you?
Bonus!
BUZZ SIGN
Talking takes money

IGNORED

Did I tell you about that top I wore on friday night?
TIMPSON
BUZZ SIGN
You spend more money...

WELCOMED

...if people speak to you

Has she spent all your money or have you got some left to spend with me?
TIMPSON
BUZZ SIGN
Talking makes the job fun

HELLO
WELCOME
WHAT WOULD YOU LIKE
BUZZ SIGN
Everyone can learn to talk

Make them feel special

We have a special price list for happy customers!
TIMPSON
NOTE
WE LIKE COMICS!
BUZZ SIGN
Make THEM smile!

TIMPSON
TIP
CUSTOMERS LIKE TO CHAT
I used to have my shoes repaired by another shop by a man called Chesterton, until he retired. Then two new men took over. But they were never polite so I decided to try Timpson...
BUZZ SIGN
LISTEN !

No problem
TIMPSON
TIP
IT'S THE ANSWER THEY ARE LOOKING FOR
BUZZ SIGN
The magic words

Dealing with a queue

TIP
LOOK EACH PERSON IN THE EYE

Getting Started

Shy people find it difficult to start talking, but anyone can learn to be even more talkative than a hairdresser. The difficult part is starting the conversation. We have a few ideas that might help.

Start a conversation

1	FOOTBALL	"Did you see the match?"
2	SOAPS	"Will you be watching Eastenders tonight?"
3	THE NEWS	"Is there anything on the news about the rail crash?"
4	TGIF	"Are you going to get your feet up this weekend?"
5	SHOPPING	"Have you been in the new Debenhams?"

BUZZ SIGN

10 topics to talk about

6	WEATHER	"It's bound to rain tomorrow, it's my day off?"
7	KIDS	"How old is she?"
8	WORK	"Are you having a busy week?"
9	HOLIDAYS	"Have you been to Spain?"
10	SCHOOL	"When do they go back to school?"

THESE ARE GREAT OPENING REMARKS

Queue Barger

Don't let your 'phone jump the queue. Customers in the shop come first, if a customer is on the 'phone politely point out you are already serving a customer and you will speak to them as soon as you can.

Caught on the 'phone

Internal Calls

No call from the office is as important as the customer in your shop. Finish any business call as soon as you see a customer needs to be served.

Caught on the 'phone

Don't say that

Some words are guaranteed to put customers off. Don't let yourself down, keep well clear of these killer comments and concentrate on the winning words which appear on the next few pages.

Killer comments

Winning words

This is what I can do for you...

This will extend the life of your shoes...

TIP

ALWAYS GIVE A REASON FOR THE EXTRA JOB

TIP

TAKE CHARGE OF THE SALE

How many do you want?
Is it for a patio door?
I'll do you a deal...
An extra key is half price...

Key words

The heels are free if...

I'll do it straight away...

I would have the stick-on sole...

This is our hardwearing sole...

Repair words

Engraving words

BUZZ SIGN

Watch words

Let me explain what this does...

What is it for?

How many eyelets do they have?

Shoe care words

TIMPSON
BUZZ SIGN
Get out from behind the counter

Self Assessment

Here is a way that you can rate your salesmanship. The better you talk the better you will do.

LEVEL		COMMENT	BONUS
0		Say nothing.	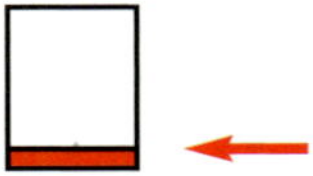
1		"Do you want another key?"	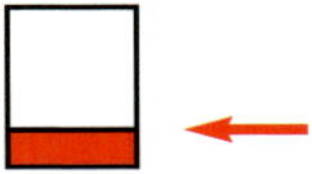
2		"4.00 for 1 6.00 for 2..."	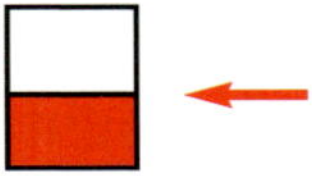
3		"Extra keys are half price."	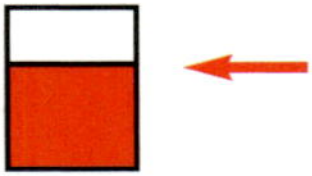
4		"How many do you want... we have a special offer on..."	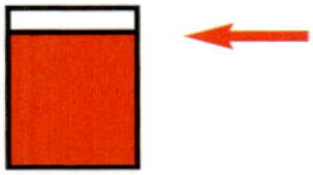

BUZZ SIGN

Rate your salesmanship

Name your price

We are probably the only multiple retailer that gives staff the authority to change our price list. Our jobs vary so much we can't set a fixed price for everything. We can only provide a guide. This level of freedom gives staff the opportunity to pick the right prices for their customers and brings a real benefit to the shop bonus.

It is only a guide

Level
3
TIMPSON
I'll give you a proper price for a proper job!
BUZZ SIGN
Quality + Proper Price = GOOD

BONUS... but Cut Price = <u>NO</u> BONUS

Fair Value

Despite the flexibility we give each branch, the price for some jobs tends to remain the same wherever you are. For a standard task, like a pet tag or house sign, there is no need to stray from our price guide.

WATCH STRAPS

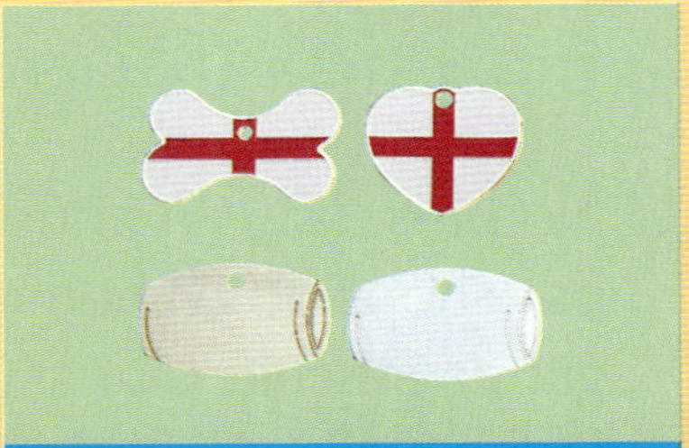

PET TAGS

BADGES

HOUSE SIGNS

Standard prices

Special Jobs

No price list can anticipate the wide variety of jobs our shops do. When it comes to watch repairs, and gift engraving. Our staff must price every job individually. All we can provide is a price guide.

WATCH
REPAIRS

CUSTOMERS
OWN ENGRAVING

Individual prices

Consumer Protection

Although we can't set specific prices, we can still protect our customers. There is a maximum price for every type of job. It varies according to the value of the article and the skill of the employee. We expect to charge a proper price for a proper job, but we should never rip off our customers.

MAXIMUM PRICES

VALUE OF WATCH ↓	SKILL LEVEL 1	2	3	4
£50	9.99	11.50	12.99	14.99
£150	12.99	14.99	15.99	16.99
£400	X	15.99	17.99	19.99
£1000	X	X	19.99	25.99

Maximum prices

WE CAN CHARGE A PROPER PRICE BECAUSE...

WE CAN CHARGE A PROPER PRICE BECAUSE...
WHILE YOU WAIT SERVICE
Can you give me 10 minutes, please take a seat.
BUZZ SIGN
We do it straight away

WE CAN CHARGE A PROPER PRICE BECAUSE...
TIMPSON
BUZZ SIGN
We work in sight

WE CAN CHARGE A PROPER PRICE BECAUSE...

John Timpson

GUARANTEED

BUZZ SIGN

We guarantee every job

Big hitter tips

We have noticed the biggest bonus earners get the best average price and wondered why. Having studied the star performers in action, we compiled a list of hot tips that would help everyone else.

Another good bonus week!
TIMPSON
BUZZ SIGN
What big bonus earners do

Talk to the customer

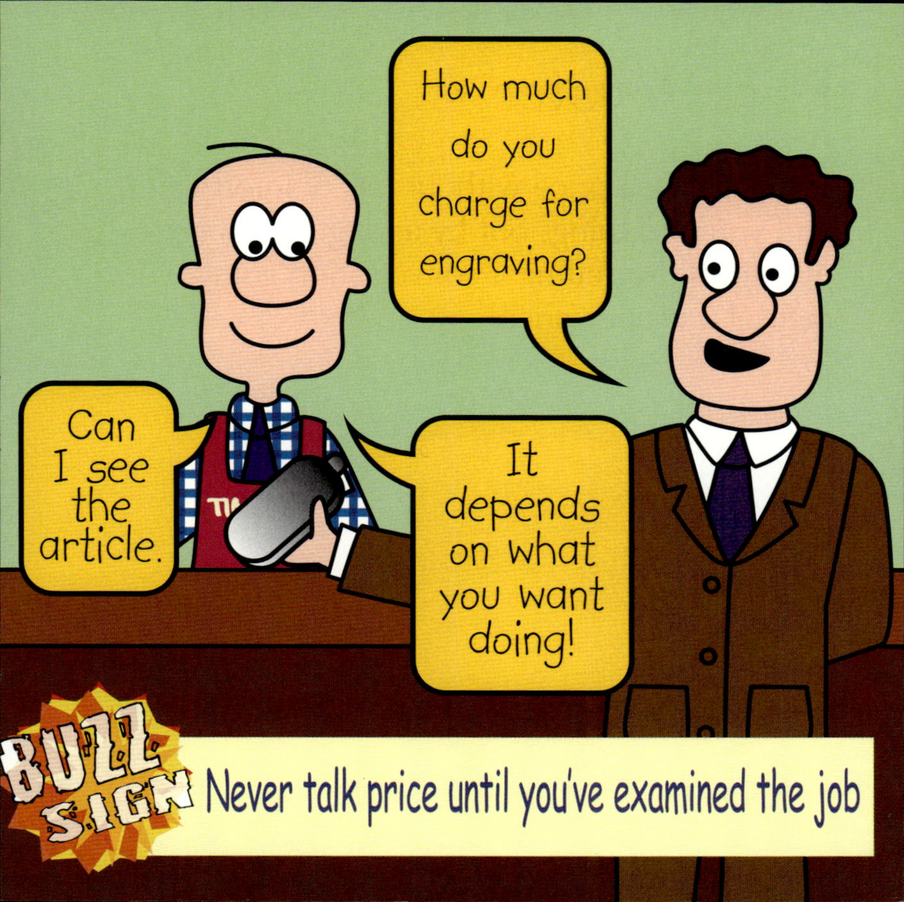
How much do you charge for engraving?
It depends on what you want doing!
Can I see the article.
BUZZ SIGN
Never talk price until you've examined the job

Price Master

You can't fix a price without lots of information and you find things out by asking customers questions. By getting a conversation going, you can set a proper price.

Has it been repaired before?
Do you know its value?
What's the occasion?
Do you have a budget?
BUZZ SIGN
Ask lots of questions

What's it worth

The value of the article for engraving or the shoes for repair will influence the price the customer is willing to pay. Don't forget if things go wrong, the level of compensation to satisfy a complaint will depend on the value of the item.

BUZZ SIGN
Value the job

VALUE OF ARTICLE

HOW LONG IT WILL TAKE

PEAK TIME PRICING

EMERGENCY

Things to consider...

THEIR BUDGET

CUSTOMERS EXPECTATIONS

SPECIAL PROBLEMS

Don't Rush

The longer you take valuing a job, the more likely the customer will accept the price you offer. Quick prices quoted without thinking are likely to be challenged, take your time and give pricing the thought it deserves.

BUZZ SIGN

Take time

Show Off

Customers like to be served by an expert. Show off your skills and give them the confidence that the job is about to be done by an expert, then they will be happy to pay a proper price.

I had one like this last week...
The movement is made in Milan.
BUZZ SIGN
Show your expertise

Here are some I did this morning.
This is the typeface you should use.
You can see it better on the screen.
2nd August 2000
Best Friends For Life
From Both Of Us With Thanks
Fluffy
TIMPSON
BUZZ SIGN
Use visual aids

I'll put in a new battery.

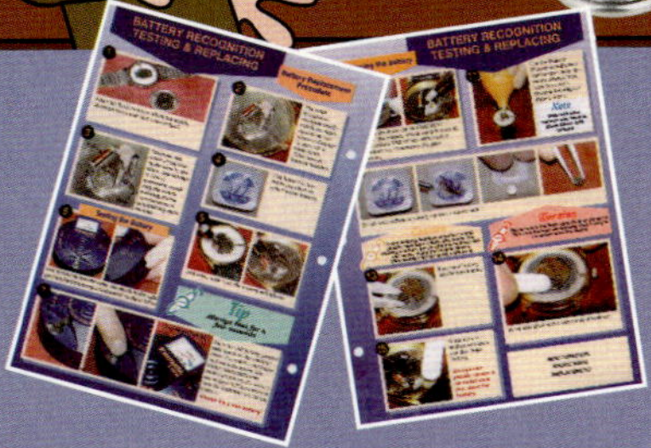

I'll show you what we do in our manuals.

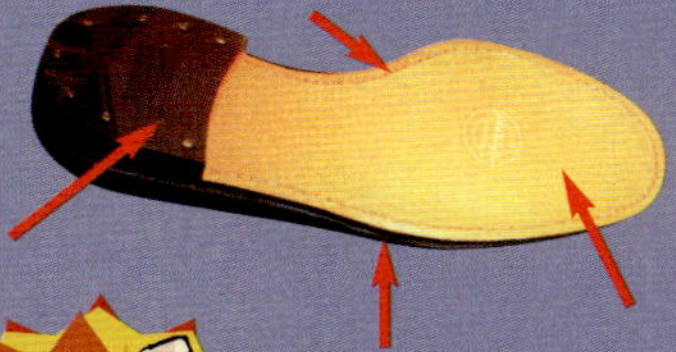

This is what it says about your shoes.

BUZZ SIGN

Use visual aids

Identity Parade

Our customers come in all shapes and sizes and bring a range of differing moods into the shop. Take notice of their character and approach the problem of pricing with their personality in mind.

MR MEAN
Expect to haggle. But be firm, he will want something for nothing!

Spot the customer

MR SPENDER

No need to haggle but don't overcharge.
He will come back again and again.

MR MESSENGER

It's not his money but he has a budget.
Find this out and work within it.

MR DITHER

Take total charge. Tell him:
"If it's not right blame me!"

Spot the customer

MR FUSSY

He is going to take time. Patience is a virtue - go with the flow and agree with him - "No problem." Price is not as important to him as you think.

MR MYSTIFIED

Not a clue - so you will make all the decisions - but make sure you give him what he needs.

MR SKINT

There is a limit to what he will pay and it isn't very much - find out what it is and then decide if you want to do the job.

Spot the customer

Take Charge

A lot of people hate shopping, they don't like making decisions. Your job is to help them. Lead the conversation and make it easy for customers to decide. It helps if you are in charge.

I know exactly what you need. It's a common problem, I can solve it!
TIMPSON
BUZZ SIGN
Lead the decision

BUZZ SIGN

Lead the decision

Most people have chosen that one.

I'm sure that's the best service.

Let's do the sole as well.

BUZZ SIGN

Lead the decision

Decision Time

You need to create a conversation to make a proper sale, but every conversation has to come to an end. It's up to you to signal when it's time to make a decision.

I think we have decided then!
OK with that?
Happy?
TIMPSON
DON'T
DON'T HESITATE!
BUZZ SIGN
Close the sale

The Works

There is always a range of jobs that can be done for any customer. Start by quoting for the full job. You can always cut a few corners and trim the price at the same time.

TIMPSON
The full service including pressure testing and battery is £18.95.
BUZZ SIGN
Quote the full job

Bargain Basement

Some customers expect to negotiate, others simply want the full job. It's important to learn how to talk price to customers. Big bonus earners are experts at haggling.

Haggle hints

I won't take less than £12.50.
TIMPSON
BUZZ SIGN
Fix a bottom price in your mind

This is how we can meet your budget.
TIMPSON
I'll tell you what I can do.
I can bring the price down if...
BUZZ SIGN
TAKE CHARGE!

Economy Drive

Under some circumstances cheap prices are justified, but only be when it's a straight forward job or you know the customer deserves some special treatment. Some times you have to drop the price to get the business, but make sure you are not giving away any bonus.

When cheap prices are justified

Children and OAP'S

MR SKINT

There is a limit to what he will pay and it isn't very much - find out what it is then decide if you want to do the job.

When cheap prices are justified

Regular customers

Quantity discounts

When cheap prices are justified

Team Work

Timpson offers the perfect example of two plus two making five. It's the dream teams that earn the biggest bonus.

BUZZ SIGN

TEAM WORK!

Odd Couples

There is no knowing who will work well together until they give it a go. If the chemistry works so well you start earning more money, you will find the friendship lasts a long time.

TRIAL MARRIAGE
TIMPSON
You never know until you try it!

It takes all sorts

Teams are not just built around skills, they depend on personality. You need people who can work together. Not just the right blend of shoe repairing and watch repair skills, but also sympathetic to each other's likes and dislikes.

BUZZ SIGN

Character counts

Must Have

All sorts of people can be successful at Timpson, but everyone needs the basic skills. They turn up on time, can do a whole range of jobs and arrive with the right attitude to work.

BUZZ SIGN

Essential attributes

Perfect Number

Get your staffing level right. Too few people on duty and you lose business, too many and the bonus scheme loses its bite. Having the right staffing level is an important ingredient of the successful Timpson shop.

BUZZ SIGN
Staffing levels

Double Success

Most successful Timpson branches are run by a team of two. They know each other well enough to raise the turnover and earn a big bonus, but they must be careful. As the business grows, they must get more help. Part-timers have an important role to play.

TIMPSON
TIMPSON
Don't forget part timers!
BUZZ SIGN
Two's company

IDEAL TEAM

BUZZ SIGN

TRUST - RESPECT -LIKE

IDEAL TEAM

He's psychic!
We have the same priorities.
He's psychic!
We have the same priorities.
TIMPSON
TIMPSON
BUZZ SIGN
Know each others next moves

IDEAL TEAM
He's best at engraving.
He's best at keys.
But we both do everything.
BUZZ SIGN
Know their strengths

IDEAL TEAM

IDEAL TEAM

SALES TARGETS
We need £2800 to beat Selfridges.
BUZZ SIGN
Bonus vultures

IDEAL TEAM

I did 20 stick on soles today - bet you a pint you don't beat me tomorrow!
TIMPSON
TIMPSON
BUZZ SIGN
Competitive

IDEAL TEAM

I'll cover for your Uncle's funeral.
You can have some of my bonus!
TIMPSON
BUZZ SIGN
LOYAL

IDEAL TEAM

I'd better do the quality jobs.
Well you do have the better skills!
TIMPSON
BUZZ SIGN
Play to your strengths

Enjoy It

Although we are in a serious business you can make it fun. Set your targets, have competitions amongst yourselves and never be ashamed of having a laugh. A happy atmosphere attracts more customers.

BUZZ SIGN

Make selling fun

Skills

Experts succeed. Your skill level has a direct effect on your ability to accumulate a big bonus. It's simple, the more you learn the more you can earn.

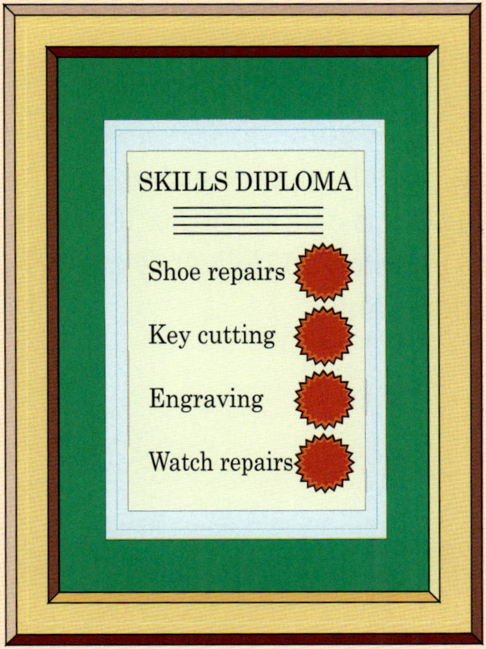
SKILLS DIPLOMA
Shoe repairs
Key cutting
Engraving
Watch repairs

BUZZ SIGN

SKILLS

"Can Do" shop

People don't just come to us for shoe repairs, key cutting, watch repairs and engraving. They often see us as the Mr Fix It of the High Street. Be prepared to deliver whatever job the customer wants.

BUZZ SIGN

Mr Fix It !!!

Admit short comings

No one knows everything so everyone still needs to learn. There is no stigma attached to admitting your failures, much better to recognise where you can improve your skills and increase your bonus.

Ask for tuition

Ambition

How good do you want to be at your job? What do you want to learn next? How can you improve the service you give customers?
If you continue to look for improvement, you will probably earn a bigger bonus.

Continue to improve

Honest Appraisal

How well do you measure up to the certificates on the wall? Can you do all the things you are meant to do? Can you remember everything you took in your skill test? From time to time, everyone needs a refresher course.

Do you need more training ?

Be honest with yourself

Q1 Do you turn any work away?

Q2 Can you talk like an expert?

Q3 Have you any skill gaps?

Ask yourself these questions

At your service

The training department is there to help you gain skills. The amount of training available to an individual is unlimited, but remember training is an individual responsibility. We wait for you to ask for training but once you have asked, we have to help.

Our training manager

Show Off

Let customers know your skills by displaying diplomas, showing our manuals and talking about training. When people come to our shop, they are buying your skills, it's important you tell them how good you are.

DIPLOMA
TIMPSON
BUZZ SIGN
Display your success

Simple Equation

It's obvious, the more things you can do, the more money you can take and the more bonus you earn. That's why skill is such an important factor in earning a bigger bonus.

More Skills

=

More Sales

=

More BONUS!

It's obvious !

'While you wait'

The magic secret of taking big money is to do every job as quick as you can. It's great for your customers and it's great for the bonus.

Why serve customers twice

As quick as you can

Quote the quickest possible time for every job and whenever there is work to be done, get on with it. Shops that don't offer 'While You Wait' lose a lot of business and miss a lot of bonus.

Always offer the quickest time...

...NEVER next week !!

Things you send away

You can't offer the St Helens and Sarsden service 'While You Wait,' but you can make sure the jobs are done as quickly as possible. Send off the order or contact Omega at once and make a note in your diary so you can monitor late delivery.

MAKE A NOTE IN YOUR DIARY AND CALL OMEGA STRAIGHT AWAY!

BUZZ SIGN

As quickly as possible

The customer is king

Whatever you are doing, customers come first. If someone wants to give you their business, don't keep them waiting. Drop what you are doing and make the sale.

Customers come first

Queue Chat

Talk to everyone in the queue and make eye contact while you do it. Top bonus earners can work and talk at the same time.

I'll be as quick as I can.
Anyone know a good joke while we are waiting!
TIMPSON
TIP
BUSY SHOPS NEED A FRONT MAN!
BUZZ SIGN
Speak to the queue

Time Machines

You should know by instinct how long each job will take. That's something that comes with experience and with it comes a bigger bonus.

That should take about 20 minutes.
It will be ready in half an hour!
TIMPSON
BUZZ SIGN
Know how long each job takes

Speed Matters

The quicker you can turn out a quality job the faster you can earn bonus. How do your best times compare with the Timpson records?

TIMPSON RECORDS

		RECORD TIME	YOUR TIME
	Two Cylinder keys	29 seconds	
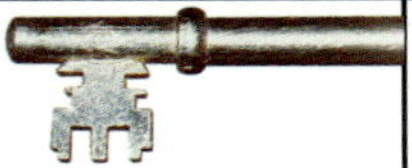	2 Mortice keys with side wards	1 minute 26 seconds	
	Long message	20 minutes	
	Pressure test	15 minutes	
	Stick-a-sole & stiletto	2 minutes 40 seconds	
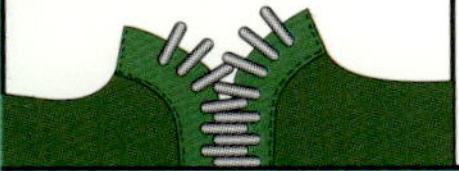	Boot zip (12")	6 minutes 9 seconds	

BUZZ SIGN

How long does it take you?

Warning Signs

You have failed the Timpson "Do it now" test if you ask customers to come back tomorrow, and the job isn't ready when they return.

Try to avoid!

Signs of success are simple

Do it quickly and have it ready when the customer returns.

Here you are, all ready!
Wow thanks!
LONGINES
ZENITH
SECTOR
BATTERIES
STRAPS
BRACELET
DIAL
GLASS
ROLEX
OMEGA
BREITLING
TIMPSON
BUZZ SIGN
Have it ready

Invisible Planning

When serving a new customer, you not only need to know what they want but also what jobs are in the pipeline. You don't plan your work schedule by computer, big bonus earners have a timetable in their mind. Their instinct sets the pace that brings them bigger bonuses.

TIP

PICTURE JOBS TO DO IN YOUR MIND

BUZZ SIGN

Mental timetable

Peaceful Activity

Find me a busy shop and it won't look busy. The cobbler who is full of shoes doesn't take much money, it's the one who has already done the work that puts the money in the till.

TIMPSON
BUZZ SIGN
Busy shops don't look busy

Everyone's Friend

We don't advertise but most people have heard who we are. Presence on the High Street doesn't just rely on the look of our shops it also depends on your personality.

Timpson Serving The Community
TIMPSON
NURSES
SHOPS
SCHOOLS
YOUTH CLUB
CLUBS
OFFICES
BUZZ SIGN
Good neighbour on the High Street

Word of mouth

The Timpson advertising budget is zero. We have become well known by looking after our customers. We play a vital role on the High Street. Make sure you are punching your weight in the local community.

WE DON'T
AD ERTISE

Friend next door

We depend on our neighbours for our business, so it makes sense to make them our friends. Look after your local shopkeepers, the pubs and the clubs, the schools and the hospitals, they are the people who live next door and they pay your bonus.

A local character

Information Centre

When someone pops in to ask a question or look for directions try to help. Know your local community so you can answer all the questions they ask.

CHURCH
BANK
BANK
SHOPS
SCHOOL
LAKE
POST
OFFICE
SHOPS
SHOPS
PARK
SC
BUZZ SIGN
Fund of local knowledge
BANK

VIP's

There are lots of people near you who are very useful to know. They are all people who bring you business. Some are listed on the opposite page.

Your who's who of the High Street

Local Conscience

You get a lot from the local community so it's right to put something back. Your Area Manager has a community fund to help people with special needs. It's not a lot of money but it can make a big difference. How can you put something back into your community?

£500
FUND
Area community fund

Service Providers

Jewellery and Shoe shops are our most important neighbours. They are the ones who provide the most business. To earn a big bonus make sure they are your friends.

Key Neighbours

Go Fishing

If you ask the right questions your customers will help you develop the business. Who else do they know that will spend money at Timpson? Are they members of clubs? Do they go to pubs? Where do they work? Do they play regular sport? Are they nurses who need badges or firemen that are down at heel? Be nosey and talk to your customers, they could lead you to a lot more business and a bigger bonus.

EXPERT WATCH REPAIRS
ROLEX
OMEGA
LONGINES
ZENITH
FREE
TIMPSON
Where do you play?
BUZZ SIGN
Be nosey

Amaze your neighbours

There are lots of things you could do to show you are not an ordinary shop, because you offer something special. Make a fuss of your neighbours and they will bring you business and add to your bonus.

Give out discount cards

Throw a party!

Send a Xmas Card

Have an OPEN DAY!

TIMPSON

WEEKLY NEWS

MORE NEW SHOPS

15 more refits are planned during March & April

Give them a newsletter

BUZZ SIGN

Do something special

In the news

Most local newspapers are desperate for news. Look how many pages are filled by the Women's Institute and the local scout pack. You have a much more exciting story to tell, but it won't get printed unless you tell the reporter. Become your own PR agent and let your local paper spread your good news and help increase your bonus.

BILL WINS
COMPANY CUP!
I'll have to call the Reporter!
BUZZ SIGN
Be your own PR agent

Community Quiz

Here are a few questions to test how much you are involved in the local community.

1. What are the names of the local jewellery shop managers?

2. Which are the four nearest hospitals?

3. How many local golf clubs can you name?

Community quiz

4. Who engraves trophies for the darts league?

5. Where are the local council offices?

6. Who are the local estate agents?

...test your knowledge!

7 Which are the five biggest local employers?

8 How many shops within one mile sell shoes?

9 Where is the nearest pet shop?

How did you do?

In branch assessment

The tips in this book are so important they will form part of a skill diploma. The skills can only be assessed by someone spending time in your branch. We think, it's important people can demonstrate their expertise by showing how they perform in front of a customer. The inconvenience of someone looking over your shoulder will be justified when you develop methods that earn a bigger bonus.

Skill assessment

New tricks for old dogs

Some people reach their peak at an early age and become complacent, others are never satisfied and always look to do better. These are the ones that earn the biggest bonus.

Even Tiger Woods has to practice!
PRACTICE GROUND
You can always get better

Recognition

In branch assessment will be part of a Management Diploma - this will help you to develop your skills and increase your bonus.

BUZZ SIGN Management Diploma

The ultimate test

John and James have favourites, they like anyone who takes big money and makes good profits. The figures matter, they are a good indication of individual ability. While we are talking of figures what's the highest amount of money you yourself have taken in a week?

Check the figures

What we look for

Every day colleagues demonstrate their ability to increase sales and earn a bigger bonus. The following pages list the things to look for.

Important signals

WHAT WE LOOK FOR

Talking to customers

WHAT WE LOOK FOR

Take time

Quote the full price first

Good at haggling

Pricing

WHAT WE LOOK FOR

WHAT WE LOOK FOR

WHAT WE LOOK FOR

WHAT WE LOOK FOR

WHAT WE LOOK FOR

Dealing with a queue

WHAT WE LOOK FOR

Skill levels

Lost sales

Maximum while you wait

(Are jobs ready on time!)

BUZZ SIGN

SIGNS OF SUCCESS!

Feedback

At the end of the assessment you will get a frank report on your performance. Praise or criticism nothing will be held back, and if necessary, arrangements will be made for a follow up visit.

Debriefing

The last word

This book describes lots of secrets that can bring you a bigger bonus but we haven't mentioned one of the most important attributes you can bring to the job - hard work. But, the smarter you are, the easier the job becomes.

PLUS

Hard Work!!